PRAY

Rev J Martin

DEDICATION

I dedicate this book to my family, for their constant love
and support.

CONTENTS

ACKNOWLEDGMENTS

This book would not have been possible without the support and encouragement of my family, and the inspiration from my Heavenly Father.

A special thanks to: my editor; Pixal Design Studios for the design work, and Amazon for providing the digital tools by which I can get my message out into the world.

Finally, I would like to thank YOU, for buying my book, may it enlighten your life and bring you peace.

Finding the Key

Never have I seen so much uncertainty in the world. So much fear, so much anger, and so much doubt. Never has there been a time that prayer is needed more than today. But to many, prayer is a mystery. What is it, exactly, and does it work?

When I was growing up, prayer was the cornerstone of life. You prayed in the morning and then had family prayer at night. Attending Church was a must. Direct communion with God each week created a happiness in your heart that never left.

How times have changed. I can only share my opinion, but with the rise of technology and easy access to the Internet, people have lost their way. Everyone is suddenly an expert, on everything; it's as if Google has taken away all the wonder, mystery, and respect in the world.

In my youth, I respected my parents; I listened to what they had to say. They might not have had access to the Internet, but they had a reference guide far more reliable? Experience. Their parents had lived through a pandemic and two world wars. So they knew how essential prayer was, and they passed that knowledge onto their children. Who in turn past it onto me.

Nowadays, people don't pray unless there is something wrong. And even then, they have never been taught how to make a connection with God.

Earlier this year, I was talking to a small business owner called Olivia, who was feeling overwhelmed with the lockdown. She was passionate about her business and truly believed in what she was doing, but fear got the best of her. She started to ask questions like, what if my business fails? What if no one wants to buy from me? What if I don't make enough money to pay my bills? Although she knew that worrying would not help, she couldn't help it. Olivia found it hard to control her negative thoughts.

Then at her lowest point, she remembered her childhood and how her mother would always take time to pray. After praying, Olivia said she did feel calmer; but the negative thoughts soon returned. So I shared with her the method of praying that changed my life.

Within a few weeks, she had regained her confidence, and the negative thoughts were gone, replaced with new ideas and faith. Which allowed her to expand her business offering online and delivery services. The next time we met, she thanked me for giving new life to her business, but I reminded her that she was the one that made it possible. All I did was show her the door; she was the one that had to walk through it.

The benefits of prayer are wonderful, but many don't experience the results they desire. And the reason for this is simple; there is so much more to prayer than a series of words. The way that you approach prayer makes all the difference. When you remove all the negative feelings that stand between you and God, your prayers contain power. Power to lift your worries, ease your burdens, and unshackle you from all your fears.

When you learn what most people never learn about prayer, you will begin to see small miracles in your life.

Why is Prayer So Powerful?

Once upon a time, there was a Welsh woman who lived in an isolated part of Wales. She went to a great deal of trouble and expense to have electrical power installed in her home.

But, after a couple of months, the electric company noticed that she didn't seem to be using much electricity. Thinking there was a problem they sent out an engineer.

When they called at her house, to their surprise, she said that she was satisfied. Saying, "we turn on the electric light every night to see how to light our lamps, then we switch them off again.

The question arises, why did this woman not make more use of her electricity? She believed in electricity, she believed in the promises the electric company told her about it. But she didn't understand the potential of electricity, what it could do for her home. And because of that, she didn't use much power. I suspect some people use prayer in the same way. They believe in the potential of prayer; they are aware of the promises God has made. They may even have read countless stories about answered prayer, but they choose to use prayer sparingly. And the reason for this is that most people don't understand how prayer works, or they think that it doesn't matter whether they pray or not.

In their heart of hearts, they don't think that prayer can make that much difference— for two reasons. They believe that God is going to do what God is going to do, so why bother? They regard prayer as a last resort, something to do after all their other efforts have failed. What needless worries we carry, all because we do not pray. All because we do not know how prayer works.

Prayer 101

How you think determines how you feel. If you choose to think negative thoughts, those thoughts will expand the more attention you give them. What started as a small problem can soon grow into something that can seem out of your control.

When caught up in negative thinking, it can feel impossible to be faithful and optimistic. People can tell you all will work out, but you will not believe them. What is important to remember when fear has control over you, is the number one rule of the mind — the mind can only think of one thought at a time.

An example, try to plan the rest of your day while thinking about what you did yesterday?

Try now.

(PAUSE)

It's impossible. Why prayer is so powerful is because it interrupts the negative thought loops that can develop in our minds—reminding us of the unlimited power and love of God.

We like to make a small action, like making a phone call into something that causes us to feel anxious and unable to eat or sleep. There is an analogy that is often overused because it is so true. If you don't weed your garden, the weeds will take it over. That's a fact. Similarly, if you don't spend time each day in prayer, focusing on the goodness of God, fear will take over. So, if you are feeling fearful, worried, or anxious at the moment, I recommend the following exercise.

Sit down with a pen and paper and write out what is on your mind. All the negative thoughts that are making you feel the way you do. Often you will find that it's only one or two things robbing you of your happiness.

Example One

I am concerned over current events, and the anxiety is taking over me. Plus, on top of that, I also feel annoyed with myself because I know that I should have better faith.

If this is a thought that is playing in your mind daily, can I encourage you to turn that thought into an encouraging prayer? So, when the negative thought comes cancel it out by saying:

Please God, strengthen my faith and make me stronger. Guide me to read the Bible more, and consume content that builds me up, and helps me to see the good in humanity.

Example Two

At this time, I am concerned about my health and the health of my family and friends. Feelings of worry and fear take over me often, and I find it hard to see how things will get better.

If this is a thought that is playing in your mind daily, can I encourage you to turn that thought into an encouraging prayer?

Dear Lord, keep my family and friends safe and healthy, both mentally and physically. Help us all to be more faithful and not let fear rob our joy.

Like weeds, negative thoughts will come, but when they do, you have to turn them around. When you put your innermost feelings in the form of prayers, they are the prayers that have the most power.

"An important point I would like to mention, from studying psychology, only use my examples as a guide. When you write your thoughts down in a structured manner, that prayer has incredible power. And the reason for this is that when YOU, restructure YOUR negative thought into a positive statement, and say it, it builds faith."

Man Has a Vision of God

There once was a weak and sickly man who lived deep in the woods in an old log cabin. He couldn't afford to go to see a doctor, and his condition seemed to be getting worse. One night while drifting off to sleep, he had a vision, God appeared in the room telling him to go out and push the enormous boulder that sat about 100 yards in front of his cabin. And if he pushed the rock, he would be healed.

The man got up early in the morning, and with great excitement, he went out and pushed the rock until lunch, then he rested and then pushed the rock until supper time. The dream seems so real that day after day, he pushed. Days rolled into weeks, and weeks into months. Faithfully he kept pushing against the rock, believing one day it would move and he would be healed. After five months of pushing the rock each day, the man was getting very tired, and because of his tiredness, he started to doubt his dream. He had accomplished nothing; he was exhausted; his vision began to fade.

The man sat on his porch and cried and cried; he had invested hundreds of hours into nothing. Nothing, it was all for nothing! As the sun was setting in the west, Jesus appeared in front of him.

"Son, why are you crying?" Jesus asked.

The man replied, "Lord, you know how sick and weak I am, that dream gave me false hope, and I have pushed with all that's within me for over five months, and that old rock didn't move one inch, it's right where it started."

"I never told you to move the rock; I told you to push against the rock."

"Yes, that's true, but I failed."

Jesus then asked the man to step in front of a mirror and look at himself. As an act of obedience, he dusted off his mirror and looked at himself. The man was amazed. Once so sickly and weak, what he saw in the mirror was a strong muscular man. Then the man realized that his bad cough and fever was gone. Pushing against the rock, had given him meaning and purpose. Resulting in him forgetting all about his health. The plan of God was not for the rock, but for the man.

When you pray, it might not move every problem, but with prayer, you are getting stronger mentally and physically, which will help you in so many other ways, preparing you for the next level of your destiny.

The trials, the heartaches, the disappointments, are all but part of the process. To strengthen your character, changing you in ways that you could never change on your own.

Two Things God Cannot Do

A man travelled for many weeks to see a great wise man of the east. The last part of the trip meant going deep into the desert. On arriving at his meeting with the great Master, he said. "Master, so great is my trust in God that I haven't even tied my camel to the post outside, I have left it to the care of God."

And the Master said, "Go out and tie your camel to the post you fool. God cannot be bothered doing for you what you can do for yourself."

This is very important to keep in mind when talking about prayer; God can't be bothered doing for you what you can do for yourself. Most of our problems come from not tying the camel, not doing what is necessary.

For example, if you have heart trouble, and have been advised by your doctor to eat healthier and get more exercise, but you don't do it. There is no point praying that you won't get a heart attack. If you suffer from painful legs and are asked to walk 30 minutes a day and stretch your hamstrings and you don't do it. There is no point praying for the pain in your legs to go away.

It's useless saying to God give-me, give-me, give-me, remember to go and tie that camel of yours. God cannot be bothered doing for you what you can do for yourself.

Like the guy whose beard is burning, and the people around him say, "your beard is on fire." And he says, "Can't you see me praying for rain. I'm doing something about it." You're saying, "Lord, may I see, and you've got your eyes tightly shut." It is pointless praying for things that are in your control.

The Story of Bob

A man I knew very well, for confidentiality, let's call him Bob. In his 40s, Bob started to have problems with his sinuses and chest. He went to many different doctors, to find out the reason, but no doctor could give him a definite answer. Frustrated, Bob decided to go to a spiritual healer to see what insight they might have. The healer told him he was holding onto a lot of negative energy that he needed to let go off. It turned out Bob held a lot of unforgiveness against the people that hurt him when he was a young man.

Bob found it hard to believe holding unforgiveness could cause health issues, so he dismissed the recommendations. Family and friends tried to convince

Bob to let go of past hurts, but he could not. Instead he prayed several times daily that God would cure him. Attending Church without fail. But he could never understand why his prayers were not answered. Sadly, Bob died a couple of years ago; he became so focused on his sickness that his health got worse. Finally resulting in him failing to 7stone and having a heart attack.

Bob's story is sad, but it happens all the time, people hold onto anger, bitterness, hatred for years, and it affects their health. Talk to any good doctor, and they will tell you the power the mind has over the body.

For example, if you have to attend a job interview or speak in front of a crowd. It's common to feel a heaviness in your chest or an un-comfortable feeling in your stomach. That feeling is similar to the feeling that people feel when they hold onto the hurts of the past. Now imagine having that feeling for 20-30 years!

Do you think it might affect your health? No wonder some people complain about problems with their hearts and stomachs.

When you let go of the hurts of the past, you will have a happier and healthier life. This point is a book in and of itself, but what I will say is this. A great way of letting go of past hurts, is to write out all the events still affecting you. The simple act of writing helps to remove the negative emotions that are trapped inside.

God Can't Help Robots

A robot walks into a room, and you tell the robot it's pretty. The robot will bounce around with joy. You just pushed the appreciation button. But if you press another button called criticism, the robot will fall to the ground, thinking it's not worthy of being a robot anymore.

Similar to the robot, just a few words can change our mood. We have learnt the bad habit of giving others total control over how we feel, meaning we are happy one minute and sad the next.

Praying when people hurt or annoy you, saying, "Dear Lord, in the future, please let people only press the buttons that make me feel good." God does not hear these types of prayers. God does not listen to robots; let me explain.

You and I as children were given a drug, and the drug was called approval, appreciation, praise, acceptance, popularity. Once you got hooked on the drug society could control you.

You became like a robot, getting stressed, depressed, and anxious just because some person or persons said a few negative words about you.

Then deprived of their acceptance, it's easy to become angry, annoyed, or upset. "Why can't I be as beautiful, as talented, as popular as everyone else. So, you seek out the drug called encouragement, praise, and belonging. Society has got us so nicely controlled.

You think Jesus was controlled by what people thought and what people said about him? Awakened people break out of this addiction, break out of needing the good opinion of others. Breakaway from being a copy, break away from being so easily controlled.

Tell the robot, "*I like you*," and the robot will automatically react. "*Yes, he's good, he likes me.*" Then say, "*I don't like you*," and the robot will automatically react. "*He's awful he doesn't like me*," — the drug.

It's the addiction to this drug that separates us from God. We doubt our abilities, judging every response we receive. And based on how others treat us, we can think we are not good enough, not pretty enough, not successful enough, even, not spiritual enough.

Want to get rid of the drug? Want to be more in control of your feelings and emotions? Well, you have to tear those tentacles out of your system. The power that society possesses over you has got to the marrow of your bones.

Like with a lot of change, the first step is awareness. It will help if you become aware of the power the drug has over you. At first, this is difficult; it's like asking a drug addict to swap his drugs for clean water, nourishing food, and daily exercise. Give up the drug for that; he can't even conceive of it.

You have to understand what your drug is doing to you. Think of your own life, is there a day when you're not consciously aware of what others think? What might they say about you if you do A B or C?

When we live to impress others, we are a slave to them; we are marching to the beat of their drum. The sad truth is, there are not too many people free from these types of feelings. Everywhere you go, you will find people wrapped up in what others think of them—living out their lives to impress others, seeking their attention and their approval.

They might gain the world, as in, material things, but they will have lost their souls. And if the attention and approval ever stop, they will fall flat on their face.

Invisible Control

Once there was a camel owner travelling across the desert, who stopped to pitch a tent for the night, and the slaves came into report that they had 30 camels and only 29 pegs to tie them too. Asking. "What would they do?"

So, the Master said to them, "you know these camels are stupid creatures, go through the motions of putting in a peg and tieing the last camel to it, and it will stay put the whole night. Which is what they did, and to their surprise, it worked.

The next morning when they were moving on, the slaves came to report that the 30th camel wouldn't budge. "Ahhh," said the Master. "You probably didn't go through the motions of untying him." So, they untied him, and the camel went with the others. Human beings are very similar. So easily contained by the good opinions of others. So afraid to move in case they are judged, in case people make fun of them for doing something different. If you can understand this, that understanding will melt the addiction, and you will be free, discovering a genuine connection to God. Because you will have dropped out of the biggest illusion of all— that you need to be appreciated, be popular, succeed to be happy.

There is only one need, and that need is to feel Gods love for you. And His love begins when you accept that you were created perfect in every way, born with unique talents and abilities. When you discover that love, your life will be transformed, and life becomes a prayer.

Why Prayers Go Unanswered?

There're many different reasons that prayers go unanswered. Most of which are out of our control. But it's the reasons that are in our control, that I would like to discuss, as they build on the foundation set in the last chapter.

There are many barriers that we put between us and God, that are in our power to remove. One of these barriers is the judgements we hold onto. How many times in the Bible does it say not to judge? That God is the only judge? Countless.

To judge is natural, we can either think something is right or wrong, good or bad, fair or unfair etc. The problem only arises when we react and respond to our judgements when we become connected to how they make us feel. For example, someone says something to you that you know is wrong, if you allow your emotions to take control, you may, "put them in their place," as the saying goes. But then your response gets the other person annoyed, and the cycle continues often spiraling out of control.

Marriages, friendships, and relationships have ended this way; one person lets their need to be right take over; leading to break-ups, arguments and fights.

We can so quickly become attached to our judgements; what we think is happening, what we believe is right; what we believe is fair. That we will dismiss everything that disagrees with our judgement. We can even become annoyed or angry with anyone who doesn't hold the same view as us.

Worse still we can judge ourselves, thinking we are not intelligent enough, beautiful enough, successful enough, popular enough, and the list goes on.

When you go beyond the judgements, beyond right and wrong, beyond good or bad, beyond happy or sad, then your prayers will connect with God, and you will feel free, expanded and safe.

The Most High created us perfect in every way, yet many of us choose to focus on the imperfections? The imperfections of others and even more damaging, the imperfections with ourselves.

If you want something from God, you have to show that you are happy with what you have already been given. If you give someone everything and they didn't show gratitude, would you provide them with anything else?

Taking Control

There once was a young man who wanted to be more spiritual. Many people advised him that the secret was to spend long sessions in prayer. But he couldn't find the time. Finally, one day he booked a day off work and had the house to himself.

Just as he was getting deep into prayer, the door knocked. At first, he ignored it, hoping they would go away, but the knocking persisted. Then someone shouted through the letterbox, "anyone home, I need a signature."

Frustrated, he got up, opened the door, signed for the box slamming the door without saying a word. Remaining angry at the driver for the rest of the day. He had completely missed the point of spirituality at the mercy of his emotions.

Like this young man, our emotions can so quickly take control, which means that when we go to pray, we hold negative feelings, like doubt, fear, or anger in our hearts. Then we wonder why our prayers are not answered?

Many people think they can live in doubt and live a life of faith. That they can hold onto the bitterness, the resentment, the unforgiveness, and get what they want.

Matthew 6:12

And forgive us our sins just as we have forgiven those that have sinned against us.

You have probably heard countless times, that holding onto un-forgiveness, pain, anger, resentment, doesn't hurt the other person it only hurts you. And maybe you have thought to yourself, "but I can't forgive them for what they did to me."

Well, if you don't forgive, the wound will never heal. In ten years, the hurtful feelings will feel as raw as ever. They hurt you once, please don't allow them to continue to hurt you again and again, for years. Your peace of mind is far too important.

(If you have been hurt and find it hard to forgive, then let your prayer be to give you the strength to forgive.)

When we feel hurt, it's often for a reason; it could be to make you move away from a particular person. It could be to teach you how not to raise your children or how not to treat others. Many people that have difficult childhoods go on to do social work to help others, so they don't go through the same pain.

Being hurt never feels good, but by holding onto the pain, you stop your spiritual growth and give God the message. "I need you in certain areas of my life but not now. I will take care of a certain person or persons in my own way." And the cost of having this attitude is years of pain and unhappiness.

For our prayers to have power, they need to be said when we are unshackled from the past; when there's no blockage from negative emotions. Our prayers need to come from a place of love.

The Secret to Effective Prayer

In the Gospel of Luke, Jesus told his disciples a parable to show them that they should always pray and not give up.

Jesus did this because He knew there would come a time when his disciples would want to quit praying. He wanted to encourage them to keep on praying no matter the circumstances they found themselves in, and this is what we should do also. Regardless of the problems we face, we should always pray. God's word tells us that in this life, we will have some trouble, but we cannot let this stop us from living.

If we want our faith strengthened, we must be prepared to take from God's hands the means for strengthening it. We must allow Him to educate us through the difficulties, problems and troubles of life. We must keep moving and persevere in prayer, even when it feels like nothing is happening. We must put our faith and trust in God and believe He is working everything out for our good.

Jesus went on to tell his disciples the parable about the persistent widow, who would not take no for an answer. Each day she went to the judge, asking him to give her justice and legal protection. The judge kept telling her no every time she asked him to help her. This was a judge who did not fear God, and he had no respect for anyone (Luke 18:2). He did not care about getting her justice, but her persistence caused him to help her. He did not help her because it was the right thing to do; he helped her because he was tired of her bothering him.

In Luke 18:4-5 he says to himself, "Even though I do not fear God nor respect man, yet because this widow continues to bother me, I will give her justice and legal protection; otherwise by continually coming she will wear me out."

Just like the widow, we need to persevere. We must pray and keep on praying. If an unjust judge would grant the widow her request because of her persistence, how much more will our loving father God give us if we are persistent in prayer.

The next time you get on your knees to pray; believe that God hears your cries, your pleas, and he will work everything out for your good.

Don't stop praying for your friends and family's salvation. Don't stop praying for healing, deliverance, relationships, and peace. Don't stop praying until God answers your prayers. Be persistent until your breakthrough comes, aware that sometimes answers can come in ways that you don't expect.

Never Give Up

There was a 4-year-old boy who went to the grocery store with his mother. Before they entered the store, she said to him, "You are not going to get any Haribo sweets, so don't even ask."

She put him in the trolley, and he sat quietly while she wheeled down the aisles. Everything was going well until they came to the treats section. He saw the sweets that he liked, and he stood up and said, "Mom, can I have some Haribo?" She said, "I told you not even to ask. You're not going to get any at all." So, he sat back down.

They continued down the aisles, but in their search for certain items, they ended up back in the treat's aisle. "Mom, can I please have some Haribo?" She said, "I told you that you couldn't have any. Now sit down & be quiet."

Finally, they were approaching the checkout lane. The little boy sensed that this might be his last chance. So just before they got to the line, he stood up on the seat of the cart & shouted in his loudest voice, "In the name of Jesus, may I have some Haribo?"

And everybody round about just laughed. Some even applauded. And, due to the generosity of the other shoppers, the little boy & his mother left with ten bags of Haribo. The little boy's persistence paid off.

We also ought to pray and not give up. But why? Why should we always pray and not give up? I mean, is God deaf? Is it hard to get His attention? Do we have to keep bothering Him until He throws up His hands in disgust and says, "If I don't grant their request, I'll never get any rest?"

No, God does not work in that way.

Very often, however, He allows us to experience things to change us and to build our character. Remember, we are supposed to be striving each day to be more like Jesus. If we never had to wait, we would never learn patience; if we didn't have to pray continuously, we might never appreciate the breakthroughs when they come. If we never experienced failure, we may never know what it means to succeed.

So, if you feel like you're not making much progress in a particular area of your life, it can help to take a step back and look at the problem or difficulty differently. Is the delay, the disappointment, or the setback giving you a message that you're failing to see?

The Only Prayer You Will Ever Need

George Muller pastored his first Church in 1830, at the age of 25. He then began his ministry five years later, helping orphaned children.

Within just a few years, thousands of orphans in Ashley Down, near Bristol, England, experienced a better quality of life, directly because of Mr Muller's work. He learned through many years to trust God for his provision.

Once asked if he found the Lord faithful to his promises, Muller without hesitation said, "Always. For nearly seventy years, every need in connection with my work has been supplied." He was well known for his powerful prayer.

Talking to a friend, Muller emphasized his dependence on God for help, by saying, "During all these years I have put my trust in God for help, in the living God, and in Him alone. We have needed as much as $250,000 in one year, and the funds have always arrived when needed. No man on earth can say that I have ever asked him for a penny. All has come in answer to believing prayer."

George Muller, a man of deep faith, died at the age of 93. He gave over $407,000 to the Lord's work during his lifetime.

Once while travelling by ship, to speak in Quebec for an engagement. He informed the Captain that he needed to arrive in Quebec by Saturday afternoon.

The Captain replied, "That's impossible, do you know how dense this fog is?'"

"No," Mr Muller answered, "my attention is not on the density of the fog, but on the living God who controls every circumstance of life. I haven't broken an engagement in 57 years; let us go down into the chart-room and pray."

Which they did.

In the chart-room, he knelt and prayed a simple prayer. When he had finished, the Captain was going to pray, but he put his hand on his shoulder and told him not to.

Saying, "As you do not believe God will answer, and as I believe He has, there's no need for you to pray about it."

Going on to say, "Captain, I have known my Lord for 57 years, and there has never been a single day when I have failed to make a connection with Him. Get up, Captain, and open the door, and you will find that the fog has gone."

The Captain opened the door, and to his surprise, the fog indeed was gone, and on that Saturday afternoon George Mueller kept his promised engagement."

The prayer that George Mueller used on the boat that day has rarely been put in print. But was revealed to me at a difficult time in my life, I was at rock bottom, I had lost my business, and felt deeply anxious about what the future would hold. I was willing to do whatever it took to see a change in my life. If it worked many miracles for him, I thought I would give it a go.

Within a few weeks of saying the prayer, my anxiety was gone, replaced with a clear vision of what I needed to do. Not only were my troubles eased, but I had a new confidence that gave me the courage to fly to South America to volunteer with street children, on my own, which led to living a spiritual and rewarding life.

Today I have hope. I feel happy and healthy, and I can only attribute it to this wonderful prayer. But before I can share the prayer, I first need to explain his method of praying, as its equally as important.

The first step is to strip back all the layers of negativity, getting to the core of who you are. Throwing off the need for approval, for acceptance, removing all the layers of judgment, the layers of anger, and any anxious or depressive thoughts. Being grateful every day for all the things you have been given. For having a healthy mind and body, and for all the beautiful relationships in your life.

It's so easy to get caught up in the meaningless, why did she look at me that way? Why did he not answer my message? Does he not like me anymore? The flesh loves the drama, the tension, the childish games. "So they think they can talk behind my back; I'm going to make them pay."

After letting go of any negative feelings, the next step is to split prayer into four stages. Pause. Rejoice. Ask, and yield.

Pause

If you rush into prayer with a bunch of requests and don't pause, then there's no adoration, there's no love and respect. It's all micro, and no macro, meaning you put yourself first, focusing only on your own life rather than looking at the bigger picture and putting God first.

The Bible says to be still and know that I am God. So, the best way to start in prayer is to stop and be still. Sitting quietly for a few moments and becoming aware of God's presence.

Often when we quieten ourselves to pray, we can become distracted by thoughts. A good exercise that works for me is to take a few deep breaths, letting any stress or tension in the body drain away.

Rejoice

When the disciples asked Jesus to show them how to pray, he gave them many instructions, one of which was the Lord's Prayer. In the Lord's prayer, Jesus starts with

"Our father who art in heaven, hallowed be thy name." Jesus showed that we must address our prayer to God as our father, to come to him with deep love and respect. It's easy to spend most of our prayer life obsessed with ourselves, all of our concerns and how we feel, and not show gratitude to our creator first. Thanking Him for everything, He has given us and humanity.

Apostle Paul instructed this, "rejoice in the Lord always, let your gentleness be evident to all; the Lord is near." Something that helps me to get prepared for prayer is to read the psalms as they put the focus on God and calm the mind.

Psalm 9:1-2
I will give thanks to you, Lord, with all my heart; I will tell of all your wonderful deeds. I will be glad and rejoice in you; I will sing the praises of your name, O Most High.

Psalm 59:17
You are my strength, I sing praise to you; you, God, are my fortress, my God, on whom I can rely.

Ask
Jesus promised, "if you ask anything in my name, it will be done for you." John 14:14. So what does "in the name of Jesus mean?"

To pray in the name of Jesus means to pray in-line with his character and his purpose. For example, not to pray for money but instead to pray to reveal the gifts that provide service to others, which in turn will give you everything you need.

In the Gospel of Matthew, chapter 7 it says, "Ask, and it will be given to you; seek and you will find; knock and the door will be opened to you. For everyone who asks receives; the one who seeks finds; and to the one who knocks, the door will be opened."

The important part of this scripture, that many overlook is that you need to keep on asking, keep on seeking, keep on knocking. As doing so keeps your attention on what you want and off what you don't, which means that you're living in expectancy, which is an essential part of faith.

When Jesus was leaving Jericho one day, a blind man called Bartimaeus was sitting on the road as Jesus was going by. When Bartimaeus heard that Jesus was coming his way, he began to shout, "Jesus, Son of David, have mercy on me. The people told him to be quiet, but he persisted. Shouting even louder, again and again, "O son of David, have mercy on me."

When he finally got Jesus attention, Jesus stopped in the road and said to the crowd, "tell him to come to me. So the people went and got the blind man taking him before Jesus. Then Jesus asked Bartimaeus, "What do you want me to do for you?" "O Teacher, he said, "I want to see." Then Jesus said, "all right, it is done. Your faith has healed you." It was clear that the man was blind as he needed to be guided to Jesus, but Jesus still wanted him to ask.

Yield

Yield is when we give way to God's will, where we surrender to what he wants to do in our life. This can often be the most challenging part of prayer because we have certain expectations. We want events to work out just the way we want. For example, you want to move to a new city, get a specific job, and then settle down, in that order. But you might meet a special person that takes your life in a whole new direction. We think we know what is best for us, but often we don't.

What many people do, however, is they don't accept God's will and keep going for what *they* want, what *they* desire, leading to unnecessary stress, disappointments and unhappiness. It's so important in life to be patient and realize there are many ways to the same destination, which is love.

When I learnt this approach to prayer, I was reminded of the prayer Jesus prayed in the Garden of Gethsemane. When He prayed, "Abba Father, everything is possible for you. Take this cup from me. Yet not what I will, but what you will." (Mark 14:36)

When Jesus says, "Abba Father," he is pausing to anchor himself in the love of God. "Everything is possible for you," After pausing, he then shows respect for God's power.' Then Jesus makes his request, "take this cup from me," as it came to the awful hour awaiting him, he didn't want to die.

"Yet not my will, but what you will." In effect, Jesus is praying for his life to be saved, but only if it was the will of God to do so.

Most Powerful Prayer

The prayer that Mr Muller used was very similar to the prayer that Jesus prayed in the Garden of Gethsemane, but he also instructed the prayer to be performed in a particular way.

Firstly, you must know precisely what you want to use it for. Any vagueness or doubt will not do. Then you are asked to kneel, stretching your arms out to shoulder height, with palms facing up. Raising your head to the heavens, then while closing your eyes, say;

Dear Lord,
I am but your humble servant.
Thank you for your wonderful creation,
of the world, and of me.

.

State your intention. Pausing, taking a moment to think of what you want; and believe that it is yours. Now taking your outstretched hands to prayer position at chest, say;

.

Help me to surrender to your will. Whatever direction that may lead. Amen.

Perform the prayer as often as you like, continuing until your request is granted.

When I started using this prayer, the first thing that I noticed was the mental shift. Preparing for prayer with intention, giving thanks to God, really focused my mind to His presence in my life. No longer was there distance, as I realized that He was around me at all times.

Very often we can get caught up with the busyness of life, so much so that even when we pray our minds are somewhere else. Unfocused prayers, as you can imagine, have little to no effect. However, when you begin to pray in the way that is outlined in this book, you will reach the highest level of prayer, which is to be prayerful.

Where you practice and live the teaching of Jesus. Showing love to everyone, forgiving quickly, and repenting when you do wrong. When you live by these three core principles, then your life becomes a prayer, and you will be in direct communion with God.

Thoughts of love, peace, and faith will fill your mind, and you will see many significant changes. You will be healthier, you will be happier, and you will have more energy. You will overcome every obstacle that stands in your way, and you will become everything God created you to be.

I would like to take this opportunity to wish yourself, family and friends. Health success and happiness in 2021.

ABOUT THE AUTHOR

I live on the northwest coast of Ireland. I use this medium to share my true voice. I wish to enlighten others and help them to see that God wants the very best for them. We often make it hard for him to enter our lives as we focus on the dark clouds rather than the silver lining.

In this growing digital frontier I just want to shed a little light out into the world to light up peoples lives in the hope that they to will help inspire others which will slowly but surely change the world, even in a small way.

My Other Books

God's Perfect Timing
The Power Of Letting Go
The Power Of Choice
The Power Of Words

Printed in Great Britain
by Amazon